# SIMON LOBDELL AND THE JUDGES IN THE CAVE

# HIDING GOFFE AND WHALLEY MAY 15 1661:
# WHAT WENT BEFORE AND WHAT CAME AFTER

**Jared Lobdell**

1

# HIDING GOFFE AND WHALLEY MAY 15 1661: WHAT WENT BEFORE AND WHAT CAME AFTER

# Introduction

Because this little book has come to have (at least) two intended audiences, it seems to me to need this introduction.

The first intended audience is made up of those interested in the hiding and pursuit of William Goffe and his father-in-law, Edward Whalley, two of the "Judges" who signed the death-warrant for King Charles I of England, executed on January 30, 1649, bringing in the "reign" of Oliver Cromwell, sometimes called the "Interregnum" because it was "between Kings" in England (1649-1660).

Cromwell, backed by his army, seized the power from the King – but the King wouldn't acknowledge that he had lost the power in the sight of God, so – to put it baldly – Cromwell had his head chopped off, and declared himself the Lord Protector of England, a term previously used when the King was an infant or small child. Cromwell died in 1658, was briefly and ineffectually succeeded by his son Richard, and then his General, George Monck, controlling the Army, brought back the Monarchy in the person of Charles II. Charles II promised a general amnesty – except for those who had voted for his father's execution, and particularly any of the "Judges" related to Oliver Cromwell.

I wrote my Junior History Paper in college on the Trial and Judgement of King Charles I, a piece of history particularly of interest to me because I grew up with English books that gave me a sentimental attraction to the "Good Old Cause" of Charles I – "For God! for the Cause! for the Church! for the laws.! / For Charles, King of England, and Rupert of the Rhine1" (But the man who wrote those words was not a Cavalier but a Whig. And Charles was not the traditionalist so much as the innovator – and inventor of Tradition.) And then I found that my immigrant ancestor seemed very much on the other side

The second intended audience, because my family is what it is, comprises those whose immigrant ancestor is the Simon Lobdell who guided Whalley and Goffe from Cambridge to their refuse in New Haven – and Milford – and New Haven – and Milford – and got them on their road to Hadley. When "the King came to his own again," Goffe and Whalley fled forthwith to New England – originally to Cambridge, in Massachusetts Bay Colony, then to New Haven and Milford (which were in New Haven Colony at that time) and then eventually to Hadley, which was in Massachusetts, but off on the frontier with the "Indians."

Here's a little background for the "Judges" of Charles I. Cavaliers (who had long hair) and "Roundheads" (Parliament supporters with cropped hair) had fought a longer (1642-46) and shorter (1647-48) Civil War in England, before Cromwell, who had led the winning side, had to decide what do with Charles, and how to do it. England was, theoretically, governed by its King-in-Parliament, but what was to be done when the King refused to call Parliament (which he did from 1629 to 1640) or when Parliament thereafter, when called, refused to acknowledge the authority of the King?

Cromwell had faced the problem of trying and convicting King Charles I for treason against King Charles I (treason in those days was personal against the King) and had put together as impressive a body of judges as he could for the put-up trial – not a very impressive lot to start with, and quite a few of them refused to sit or to judge, but in the end fifty-nine signed the death warrant, including Cromwell.

Several, including Cromwell, had died by the time Charles II came to the throne. The bodies of Cromwell, General Henry Ireton, and Chief Judge John Bradshaw were dug up and ceremonially executed. Nine of those living were executed, including Cromwell's brother-in-law, John Jones. Those who are interested in what happened to all fifty-nine may read Charles Earl Spencer's recent book, K*illers of the King: The Men Who Dared to Execute Charles I* (2014). (Earl Spencer's sister was the Lady Diana, Princess of Wales, sometime wife and consort of the presumed next King Charles of England.)

Briefly, forty-one of the fifty-nine were alive on May 29, 1660, when the King (Charles II) came "back" to the throne of his father. Of these forty-one, fifteen fled the British Isles, five to Switzerland, eight to Germany and the Low Countries, two – Cromwell's cousin Edward Whalley (1593?-1676?) and his son-in-law William Goffe (1607?-1689?) – to North America. (Eventually John Dixwell likewise came to North America, indeed to New Haven, from the Low Countries.) Three were kidnapped from the Low Countries, taken back to England, and there executed (John Barkstead, John Okey, Miles Corbet): they were betrayed by their former colleague, George Downing, who gave his residence to the Crown so the King's Minister could live there (it is now No. 10 Downing Street). Except for a few who turned their coats, or who had intervened to save Royalists in the days of Cromwell's Protectorate or of the Civil War itself, the Judges who faced trial were convicted and sentenced to death, but most were reprieved and spent the rest of their lives in some sort of sequestration.

They were in sequestration or they were in exile – and in a sense Goffe and Whalley suffered both – exile from Old England and practical imprisonment in New. And yet that isn't quite right. Goffe drilled the men of Hadley in the "Indian" War we call King Philip's War (1675-76), and Whalley apparently rose from his deathbed to lead them, however crazily, into battle. They had good, though limited, company in their New England years – even hearing a servant-woman (they said "wench") singing anti-Regicide ballads in their refuge in Milford, the singer not knowing the subjects of her song were hidden a room next to the one where she was singing.

Those who are reading this story to find out whether the pursuit for Whalley and Goffe was genuine or (as it now would be called) "fake" probably knew all this already. Those who are reading it because it was their (and my) immigrant ancestor, Simon Lobdell (1632-1717) who brought the Judges to their refuge in New Haven, and – we believe – protected them thereafter, may find too much fact here for true understanding of what happened. But as they read, one thing may be kept in mind, particularly.

Simon Lobdell held an officer's commission in a Colonial Army, but before that he was in rebellion against the Crown – but not against King Charles I personally (as Cromwell and Whalley and Goffe had been). Rather, as Ezra Stiles clearly saw, when he assembled the materials for his *History of Three of the Judges of King Charles I* over long years before its publication in 1794, in rebellion against the Crown.

Not Nathaniel Bacon in his rebellion in Virginia or Leisler in New York or the leaders of tax and other protests in the Colonies in the Eighteenth Century – but Simon Lobdell, freeman of Milford in New Haven (1656) – heads the procession that other Colonial officers and frontiersmen and just plain citizens joined a century after he was Lieutenant in Springfield in 1676 – and a century after Edward Whalley was the "Angel of Hadley" that year.

All of what happened and how it all happened is our story here. To repeat our title, "Simon Lobdell and the Judges in the Cave: Hiding Goffe and Whalley May 15 1661 – What Went Before and What Came After." I have tried to tell the seventeenth-century story in something of a seventeenth-century manner, to put it in context, at least a little. Whalley (and to some extent Goffe) grew up in Shakespeare's England, even Shakespeare's London. We believe Simon Lobdell's father fought for the Dutch against the Spanish when Elizabeth I was on the throne, and he may even been a ship's boy (on the family ship) fighting against the Armada in 1587-8, the year his father died. Our story is later, of course – but it's still seventeenth century, long long ago, when family ties pretty much ruled the Atlantic world – which is why there's a lot of genealogy in this paper.

One genealogical point should probably be covered here. Nicholas Lobdell (1578-1651?) was the younger son of William Lobdell (1536?-1588), whose elder son James had a son James (called James Lopdell, 1624-1682), who went to Ireland in 1657 as part of the Cromwellian settlement there. Another part of that settlement was John Whalley, son of the Major-General. Their children married, so that Simon Lobdell (1632-1717) was cousin by marriage (albeit once removed) to Edward Whalley's grandchild in Ireland, a connection rather than a relation, but still "family."

When Cromwell was winning the English Civil War, he had to find a way to rule over England. It was through the Army, of course, and the title "Major-General" was an administrative title, usually with a specific geographic authority (four counties in Whalley's case, three in Goffe's). The substantive military rank of a Major-General was most likely that of Colonel, so that both Whalley and Goffe were correctly both "Major-General"

Interestingly, when their military colleague, Daniel Gookin, was placed in authority in Massachusetts in time of war, his title of "Major-General" seems to have been both military and civil, but after that the title was considered simply military – in the Colonies, at least.

Jared Lobdell
Elizabethtown PA
Feast of St. Edward Confessor
October 13, 2017

# Prologue

We are asking you (quoting Elizabethan words) to entertain conjecture of a time – not when creeping murmur and the poring dark filled the wide vessel of the universe, though there was sufficient murmur and sufficient dark, but – when the universe, or at least our Atlantic world, was filled and defined by the ties of kinship and family (and network of "family friends"). We are asking you to center your consideration on one incident (or stream of incidents) in the crowded history of Seventeenth Century Connecticut – the hiding of Colonel (or Major-General) William Goffe and Major-General (or Colonel) Edward Whalley, around and about New Haven (including Guilford and Milford), in the years 1661-1664, and particularly their hiding in Judges' Cave, May 15, 1661, with those ties in mind. We shall find that these ties may help explain the lack of success in the "pursuit" of the Judges, as well as enhancing our views of the people of 17th-century Connecticut – and Massachusetts, and Virginia.

But here, before this, we can look at a scattering of events leading up to ours. Because Whalley was the senior, and Goffe's father-in-law, and Whalley was Oliver's first cousin, he is hereafter referred to as the Major-General, and Goffe as the Colonel, though both, in fact, were both, nor did either title exclude the other – and one at least was a Lieutenant-General. It should be noted that *Major-General* might be considered the administrative rank (like Lord-Lieutenant) and *Colonel* the military rank, and either could by courtesy be extended to an individual no longer actively serving as either, much as, for example, the late William Scranton [1917-2013] of Pennsylvania was called "Governor" Scranton for the last fifty years of his life, though his term as Governor ended in 1967. (He was born, by the way, in a summer cottage on family property in Madison, Connecticut, not far from where Dennis Scranton [sometimes given as Dennis Crampton], one of those who helped hide the Judges, lived in 1661.)

## The Family Story

There is in the Lobdell family a tradition of Simon Lobdell and his story of Major-General Whalley and Colonel Goffe, as it was supposedly told by his son Joshua (1671-1743), Selectman of Ridgefield, to Joshua's son Darius (1729-1796), sometime in the Legislature of the Republic of Vermont, and Darius to his son, the Reverend Jared Lobdell (1767-1846): this has served as a keynote for some of our suggestions and reconstructions. I daresay it may very well be a later reconstruction, but in any case, it seems to agree with the commonly told story, and can serve as an introduction to this paper.[1]

Here is the Lobdell family story of the guide and his Colonel and General on the path from Cambridge: Major-General Whalley and Colonel Goffe had been some months at Massachusetts Bay, at the village of Cambridge, some four miles from Boston, when there came a ship following from England with the warrant of King Charles II, for their arrest., and two "Royalists" – Captain Kellond and Captain Kirke – to search them down. It was late in February, in the year 1661 – but they called it 1660 still, for they began their years in March – Simon Lobdell, a pathman and guide, a citizen of Milford in the New Haven Colony, with Goffe and Whalley left Cambridge in Massachusetts Bay.

---

[1] The author showed a typescript copy of this Lobdell family story to Frank Bremer some years ago: it has no independent authority but seems to be in agreement with the facts as known.

14

Their destination was Theophilus Eaton's colony at New Haven, going there on the inland path through the colony at Hartford on the Connecticut, the great Bay Path to Springfield and then the River Path to the southward. The Commonwealth of New Haven outlived Theophilus Eaton by a scant five years, but this was the fourth of those five, and New Haven Colony was still independent and separate.

It was said in our family that they were merry companions, Goffe and Whalley, in Simon's four days on the path to Hartford with them and John Meigs. The path went in those days, first from the Bay to the Praying Indian towns, across the Great Indian Bridge at Natick, then into the Nipmuck country, and so to Springfield, in the Connecticut Colony, and along the river to the Hartford towns. The Great Indian Bridge was eighty feet across and built of planed planks, by the Praying Indians, from their own saw-mill.[2] Simon carried what some said was a snaphance, but perhaps it was a plain flintlock musket, and he carried also a little New England bow. So also was John Meigs armed, but the Colonel and the General carried their pistols and their swords.[3] Of snaphances or muskets they may have carried, we do not know. In the Nipmuck country, they met a hunter or two or three along the way, but these knew Simon, and besides, in those days the Nipmucks were our friends, it was said, against the Dutch at New York that was then New Amsterdam. It would have been a great sight to see the four of them at camp-fire with a Nipmuck hunter, at Quinsigamond, where Worcester is

---

[2] Daniel Gookin, *Doings and Sufferings of the Christian Indians* [1677, published Boston 1836].

[3] Patrick Malone, *The Skulking Way of War: Technology and Tactics among the New England Indians* [Lanham MD 1991].

now, snow on the ground, and the General and the Colonel telling stories.

At the close of the fourth day they were at the Hartford towns, and then southward still in the morning, and at the close of the fifth day they came within the precincts of New Haven. There they remained for several weeks, in which time Simon journeyed at least once to Massachusetts Bay and back. But toward the end of this month of March, 1661, after the New Year's Day on March 25th, he conducted them to Milford, as though to take ship to Manhattan ["Manhados"] in the Dutch country. But they went not to Manhattan, returning instead in secret to New Haven, whilst he remained in Milford. What it was that Simon did in Milford those next two weeks has not been handed down to us in any form. But it seems that while the Judges were in New Haven, and Simon was to the northward, their pursuers came from Boston, and it was therefore Mr. Jones (perhaps) and Mr. Burrill who guided the Judges to this West Rock cave that Simon knew, for hiding.

## A Vignette: Visiting the Knight of Hinchingbrooke

Properly this vignette is not strictly an event leading directly to ours, but it is a part of the background not generally regarded. We are at Hinchingbrooke House, in Huntingdon, Cambridgeshire, around 1600, with Queen Elizabeth [I] visiting her favorite Tudor [third] cousin, the Knight of Hinchingbrooke. Her host's grandson, an infant of very few years, was there at the time. Whether he was dandled on her knee, as tradition has recorded, is uncertain. His name was Oliver Cromwell. (One thing we know for sure: she never dandled Oliver's great opponent, Charles I, on her knee: she never even saw him.) There is no indication that another grandson, by name Edward Whalley, was present that time at Hinchingbrooke.

16

Joan Tudor, daughter of Jasper Tudor [1431-1495], the younger brother of Edmund Tudor 1430-1456] who was father of Henry VII, and they were half-brothers of Henry VI (on their mother's side), was the mother of Morgan ap William [Williams], who married Catherine Cromwell (born circa 1482), older sister of Thomas Cromwell. Morgan ap William [Williams], son of William ap Yevan of Wales and Joan Tudor, was thus first cousin of Henry VII (Henry Tudor). Morgan Williams took the name Cromwell, and the family line continued [1] through Richard Williams/Cromwell, (c. 1500–1544, but sometimes the date of death is given as 1533), second cousin of Henry VIII and of his sister who married James Stuart, King of Scotland; [2] through Sir Henry Cromwell of Hinchingbrooke (c. 1524/1537–6 January 1604), third cousin of Elizabeth I (and of Mary Queen of Scots), then [4] to Oliver's father Robert Cromwell (c. 1560–1617), fourth cousin of James VI and I, who married Elizabeth Steward or Stewart (1564–1654) on the day of Oliver Cromwell's birth.[4]

Oliver Cromwell was thus fifth cousin to Charles I, as well as of the Blood Royal of France (through Katherine of Valois) and, arguably, Wales. Whalley shared this heritage. During the Second Civil War (1647-48) he had been King Charles's jailer, and was thanked by the King for his courtesy. I wonder if either of them called the other Cousin.

It has been said, by the way, that Oliver had not a drop of royal blood in his veins (unlike his cousin George Monck, Duke of Albemarle, who restored Charles II, and was of Plantagenet blood through his grandfather Arthur, Viscount de L'Isle, son out of wedlock of Edward

---

[4] The 1524 date was given until very recently in *The Peerage* online: the change to 1537 is highly dubious.

IV) But Oliver did have royal blood, though he did not have Charles I's blood of Lancaster and York. But he had the same Tudor blood [though that wasn't the Blood Royal of England] and the same Valois Blood Royal of France.[5]

## A New-World Scout

The scout in question was an Englishman, in the lands between the Dutch in "Manhados" and the English at Plymouth, in the first part of the 1620s. He was a little man, as the nickname we have found for him suggests, and it is possible he was the "Little Man" who scouted westward from Manhados for the Dutch in that year of 1615 when white men first entered Pennsylvania, three men across the Delaware from Manhados, and Étienne Brulé down from Canada by the rivers, portaging to the Juniata and then down the Susquehanna. Here is the story from the debatable lands in Connecticut.[6]

"One other tradition is the following, being told in many different ways; of which we accept the simplest, as being, probably, the nearest to the truth. A rough old Dutchman named Cornelis Labden, was riding away from the settlement in Old Greenwich on horseback, when he discovered that he was pursued by three Indians on foot. They could pass more nimbly through the forest than he, and unless he could free himself by some desperate attempt, he well knew the destruction that awaited him.

"In this strait he bethought him of that steep precipice which still bears the name of Labden's Rock, and resolved rather to die by plunging

---

[4] All this from G. E. C., *The Complete Peerage*, reflected in *The Peerage* online.

[6] Dingman Versteeg, ed., *Manhattan in 1628* [New York 1904], esp. p. 140.

down its depths than by the torturing hand of the red man. Just as his pursuers were about overtaking him, he dashed over the steep, and they, too eager on their pursuit, went headlong after him. Of the whole mass of mangled flesh, Labden only lived to tell the story and that with his two legs broken. This Rock still presents much of its old appearance, and is visited by many of the curious." [7]

Now there is no record of any Labden (or Lobden or Lobdell) among the settlers of Old Greenwich circa 1640 (or any other time), nor any Lobden of any name in the area then (Nicholas was in Hingham, where his wife died in 1641, and where he signed papers in the years thereafter – and his son Simon was not yet ten years old). But let us take "Cornelius" as a folk-remembering of "Cort Niklaas" (Little Nick – he had a slightly older cousin Nicholas 1575-1621, also in the Dutch service), and "Labden's Leap" (becoming "Aladdin's Leap') as folk-remembering of "Lobden's Leap," and put the time back to a time when Nicholas could reasonably have been in the area. Nicholas seems to have left the New World about 1624-25, returned to Devon and there married a younger wife, then returned with his wife and son and daughter to Massachusetts in 1635.[8]

The record of the "Little Man" is, as noted above, found in *Manhattan in 1628*, a letter from Dominie Jonas Michaelius [1577-1642?],[9] edited by Dingman Versteeg, and published in New York in

---

[7] Daniel Mead, *History of the Town of Greenwich* [1857], pp. 39-40. Anya Seton uses a version of the story fictionally in *The Winthrop Woman* (New York 1958)

[8] Jared Lobdell, "Progress on the Dispersion of the Lobdell/Lopdell Family in the 17th Century" in *Sussex Family History* (2002), pp. 42-51.

[9] Dingman Versteeg, ed., *Manhattan in 1628* (New York 1904).

1904 His mark [as "Kleintjen"] is on the map prepared from the travels of the three men from the company (including "Kleintjen") who had been captured in the "South River" [Delaware] country by the Minquas. The Minquas were Susquehannocks or Conestoga, an Iroquois people in southeastern /south-central Pennsylvania.

The three men had gone to trade with the Mohawks (Iroquois but not close to the Minquas) and Mohicans (Algonquian people usually at war with the Mohawks), whose languages they spoke.—or at least the "Little Man" did.

The Mohawk-Mohican wars carried over into Connecticut, as late as the Judges and certainly at the time of the "Leap" as we have set it. (The "Leap" has probably been confused in folk memory with the more famous "Leap" of Israel Putnam in the same area: it is unlikely "Lobden's leap" took place on horseback.)

## Gentlemen Adventurers: the Soldier and the Ferryman

The names we think of from the early history of seventeenth century America – John Smith, Myles Standish, maybe Lyon Gardner, John Mason, Brewster, the Mayflower names, the Massachusetts Bay names of 1630, Stephen Hopkins, Winthrop, Winslow – may or may not give us men or women who are representative of the time and place, and who will help us understand it.

Before we get into the body of this paper, it may be a good thing to sketch the careers of two seventeenth-century gentlemen-adventurers – one of whom – Daniel Gookin – is emblematic of the seventeenth-century Atlantic commonwealth-man and one of whom – William Pierce – had a career casting great light of that seventeenth-century Atlantic. And both play a part in our story.

## Major-General Gookin, the Soldier

Daniel Gookin was born, perhaps in County Cork, Ireland, in the latter part of 1612, the third son of Daniel Gookin of County Kent and County Cork and his wife, Mary Byrd, and was baptized 6 December 1612 at the church of St. Augustine the Less in Bristol.[9] By 1616 his father was living in Carrigaline, Ireland, where Gookin probably spent his childhood, later being sent for education to England. On 1 February 1630/1, shortly after his eighteenth birthday (according to his generally established birth-date), he was living at his father's plantation in Virginia But this may not have been his first residence there, and we know a little more about the Gookin family of Virginia than was known when the DNB published its sketch of the life of our Daniel Gookin back in 1890. Daniel Gookin Sr. settled at what is now Newport News in 1621, and his plantation resisted successfully the great Indian attack of 1622 – Daniel Gookin Sr. being apparently the first man to reach London, and apparently leaving his son in charge – suggesting that 1612 may be too late a birthdate for our Daniel Gookin.[10] Bringing the bad news from Newport News to London was not the job for an unimportant man, and in fact Daniel Gookin Sr. may be ranked as the founder of Newport News, in addition to being one of the important survivors of 1622, and his son had an early experience of Indian warfare. It would be hard to find another survivor of 1622 fighting in King Philip's War in 1675-77.

No record of our Daniel's first marriage has been found; but on 11 November 1639 a license was granted for the marriage of Daniel

---

[9] His life is in *DNB* Vol. 22 (1890), pp. 152-164

[10] C. E. Hatch, Jr., *The First Seventeen Years: Virginia 1607-1624* [Charlottesville /Jamestown 1957], pp. 98ff.

Gookin, Gent., of the parish of St. Sepulchre, London, a widower, and Mary Dolling (but she is later called Mary Byrd), of the parish of St. Dunstan in the West, London. Between his two voyages to Virginia, it is assumed that Gookin was in military service, as he is referred to as a Kentish "souldier" by Capt. Edward Johnson in his *Wonder Working Providence*, and "Captain" in Greer's list of immigrants to Virginia. In early 1641 our Daniel Gookin, his wife Mary, and their infant son set sail for Virginia and took up residence at the Nansemond plantation. He was made a Burgess and represented Upper Norfolk County in the Grand Assembly which met in Jamestown on 12 January 1641/2. He received a grant of 2,500 acres (10 km$^2$) in the upper county of Norfolk on the northwest of the Nansemond River on 29 December 1637, and a further 1,400 acres (5.7 km$^2$) on the Rappahannock River on 4 November 1642.

His brother John died at Lynn Haven early in November 1643, and, no longer bound by any strong ties to Virginia, he left his three plantations in the charge of servants and sailed for Boston in May 1644 with his wife and his infant daughter Mary. They arrived in Boston on 20 May 1644, and six days following he was admitted to membership in the First Church. He resided initially at Roxbury, where he was a near neighbor of Rev. John Eliot, Sr., the "Apostle to the Indians". Gookin's daughter Elizabeth (baptized 1645) was later to marry John Eliot's son. Gookin was appointed a deputy from Roxbury to the General Court. On 6 April 1648 he sold 500 acres of his plantation on the Rappahannock to Capt. Thomas Burbage. In July 1648 the Gookin family removed to Cambridge, where he was appointed Captain of the Trained Band, a position he held for the next forty years. In the spring of 1649 he was chosen as Deputy from Cambridge to the General Court held in Boston.

In July 1650 he was in London on public business, returning by spring of 1651, when, on 7 May he was chosen Speaker.

At the election on 26 May 1652 he was chosen an Assistant, one of the Council of eighteen magistrates to whom, with the Governor and a Deputy Governor, the government of the colony was entrusted. Except for a period early in 1676, when he suffered defeat largely because of his sympathetic treatment of "Indians" during the Indian War, Gookin was re-elected to this position continuously for a period of thirty-five years.

In the early days of Cromwell's Protectorate, Gookin again returned to London, where his cousin Vincent Gookin was a member of the first Protectorate Parliament. He became Collector of Customs at Dunkirk in March 1658/9. When King Charles II returned to Dover, he fled to New England with Whalley and Goffe. Gookin served Cambridge as Selectman from 1660 to 1672, and was appointed the first Superintendent of the Praying Indians. In this capacity he traveled to Indian settlements, often accompanied by his friend the Rev. John Eliot. Gookin wrote two books on the Indians: *Historical Collections of the Indians in New England* (completed in 1674, published by the Massachusetts Historical Society, 1792), and *The Doings and Sufferings of the Christian Indians* (completed in 1677, published in 1836).

He wrote also a *History of New England*, only portions of which have survived. On 11 May 1681, he was elected Major-General (notice the title or rank), the Commander-in-Chief of the military forces of the colony. He died on 19 March 1686/7, and was buried in the Old Cambridge Burying Ground, the town's main burial site. We remember from President Stiles that, according to Hutchinson, Gookin was reported to "manage their [the "regicides"'] estates; and the commissioners [investigating the regicides] being informed that he [Gookin] had many cattle at his farm in the King's Province which were supposed to be Whalyes or Goughs, caused them to be seazed for his Majestyes use til further order, but Capt. Gookin, standing upon the privilege of their charter and refusing to answer before the commissioners, as soe, there was no more done in it.[11]

## Captain Pierce, the Ferryman

Experts in seventeenth century maritime history may know if the *Hector* that brought John Davenport and Theophilus Eaton to New England in 1637 was the same *Hector* that brought Major-General Goffe and Major-General Whalley and Major-General (as of 1681) Daniel Gookin (and Lieutenant-Governor William Jones) in 1660. Gookin's connection with Cromwell did not of course begin with Goffe and Whalley, as we have noted – far from it.

Of the Captain Pierce who brought the Judges over, we can say that he was most likely William Pierce (or Peirce or Purse or Percy) the younger (d. 1661), son of William, the Ferryman of the Atlantic (1590-1641). This ferryman, William Pierce (1590-1641) – son of Captain William Pierce [1560-1622] – was the most celebrated master of ships that came into the waters of New England. (Simon Lobdell married a Pierce connection: it is possible that he was named after his aunt's second cousin, Simon Hudson, also of a nautical family.)

A friend of Winslow and Bradford: William Pierce the ferryman is first noticed in the early records of the Plymouth colony in 1622, when he was master of the *Paragon*, the owner of which ship was his brother John Pierce of London. In 1623, Capt. Pierce brought over to Plymouth

---

[11] Ezra Stiles, *History of Three of the Judges of King Charles the First* [New Haven 1794], p. 60

the *Anne* with a noteworthy company. In 1624, he came in the *Charity*, conveying Winslow and his cattle, the first brought into New England.[12]

In 1625 he was at Plymouth in the *Jacob*, again bringing Winslow and more cattle. In 1629, he commanded the famous *Mayflower*, and in her he took a company from Holland as far as the Bay on their way to Plymouth; and in the next year, February 1630, he came with the *Lion* from Bristol, which was a part of Winthrop's fleet. In Winthrop's Journal, under date of Saturday (12th June, 1630), we find the following: "About four in the morning we were near our port. We shot off two pieces of ordnance and sent our skiff to Mr. Pierce, his ship (which lay in the harbour and had been there [blank] days). About an hour after Mr. Allerton came on board us, in a shallop, as he was sailing to Pemaquid." Owing to the destitution at the Bay, he was hurried back for provisions, with which he returned November 22.

November 29, 1631, he came over again in the *Lion*, and with him John Eliot and Governor Winthrop's wife. In 1632 he sailed once more to Boston and Plymouth in the *Lion*; but after carrying Winthrop to Weymouth lost his ship on the Virginia coast, for which place he sailed October 27, 1632. In 1634 he was gathering Oldham's corn in the *Rebecca*, and taking observations in the *Narragansett*, and the next year was first in the West Indies, and then later on in the Bay Colony's service, rescuing refugees from the Connecticut Valley and returning them to Boston. In 1635 Pierce's *Rebecca* of sixty tons was built at Medford. In 1636, with the fine new ship *Desire*, one hundred and

---

[12] See W. R. Cutter, *New England Families, Genealogical and Memorial*, Vol. 4, New York 1914. After the death of Pocohontas, he was John Rolfe's brother-in-law (Rolfe having married Jane Pierce, presumably the Ferryman's sister).

twenty tons, built for him at Marblehead, he went with Endicott's force to Block Island.

In 1637, he carried supplies from Boston for the soldiers of the Pequot War and acted as tender. In 1638, he sailed between Boston and the West Indies; at this time he seems to have presented Winthrop with what the latter calls an *aligarto*—an animal which much interested the Bostonians. In 1638, he cleared the *Desire* from London with passengers for Boston, from Boston keeping on to the West Indies. In 1639, he sailed the *Desire* from Boston to the Thames in twenty-three days. In 1641, he carried a party of "dissenters" to settle in the West Indies; but owing to the hostility of the Spaniards, he turned back with his passengers, and put into New Providence to bring away a congregation living there.

With the Spaniards already in possession, he stood gallantly in, hoping to rescue his countrymen. When the enemy opened upon him with cannon, he sent his people into the hold for safety, retaining on deck but one man to aid in working the ship – he and that sailor being fatally wounded by the same shot. The *Desire* was then headed for home. That Simon Lobdell's wife's first name was Persis suggests strongly her connection with the Ferryman's family, since the name is generally found only in the Pierce family and their connections.[13] (We also noted, just above, a possible connection with another English seafarer, inthis case in the Dutch service.)

---

[13] See W. R. Cutter, *New England Families, Genealogical and Memorial* [New York 1914].

# The Hiding

We have told the Lobdell family's [brief] version of this history in our Prologue. Let us look now and the tracks and trails of the pursued and the pursuers, and what manner of men they were, and what were their family connections, to see if we can understand the story better. Here is what we find on the tracks and trails of the Judges.

### Tracks & Trails: Goffe & Whalley – Guilford, New-Haven, Milford

The pursuers, Kellond and Kirke, were apparently in Guilford by May 11th, at which point the Judges shifted to "the Mill" – possibly (already) Sperry's Mill. By the time Kellond and Kirke were in New Haven, May 13th, the judges had apparently moved to a temporary lodging at Hatchet Harbor (wherever that was), and when the pursuers left New Haven (and local searchers took their place), the Judges climbed to Judges' Cave, where they remained from May 15th through June 11th. Here are the words of Kellond and Kirke.[14] on their adventures in Guilford and New Haven on the 11th, 12th, and 13th: "after our parting with [Deputy Governor Leete] out of his house and in the way to the ordinary, came to us one Dennis Scranton [Crampton?], and told us he would warrant that Colonels Goffe and Whalley at the time of his speaking were harbored at the house of one Mr. Davenport, a minister at New-Haven, and that one Goodman Bishop, of the town of Guilford, was able to give us the like account, and that, without all question, Deputy Leete knew as much, and that Mr. Davenport had put in ten pounds worth of fresh provisions at one time into his house, and that it was imagined it was purposely for the entertainment of them...."

---

[14] Stiles, *History of Three of the Judges*, pp. 52-53

"Upon [hearing this] we went back to the Deputy's and required our horses, with aid, and a power to search and apprehend [Goffe and Whalley]; horses were provided for us, but he [Deputy Leete] refused to give us any power to apprehend them, nor order any other [to help], and said he could do nothing until he had spoken with one Mr. Gilbert and the rest of the Magistrates: Upon which we told him we should go to New-Haven and stay till we heard from him, but before we took horse the aforesaid Dennis Scranton gave us information, there was an Indian of the town waiting... to give notice of our coming. But to our certain knowledge one John Megges [Meigs] was sent a horse-back before us, and ... was to give them an information, and the rather because by the delays ... it was break of day before we got to horse, so he got there before us; upon our suspicion we required the Deputy that the said John Megges might be examined what his business ... might occasion his so early going; to which the Deputy answered, that he did not know any such thing, and refused to examine him; and being at New-Haven, which was the thirteenth day, the Deputy arrived within two hours or thereabouts after us."[15]

## Tracks & Trails: Goffe & Whalley – Hatchet Harbor, Judges' Cave

Let us now try to trace out, according to tradition, "these exiled pilgrims [Goffe and Whalley] in their several retreats, migrations, and secret residences" – beginning more or less at New-Haven where they first disappeared.  Note that this entire reconstruction of where the Judges hid is based on traditions collected a hundred years after.  Here is President Stiles[16]

---

[15] Ibid.

[16] Stiles, *History*, pp. 72-75:

"They retired from town, to the west side of a rock or mountain, about 300 feet perpendicular, commonly called the West-Rock, to distinguish it from the Neck-Rock, to the N. E. of the town. The southern extremity of West-Rock lies about two and a half miles N. W. from the town. Between this, westward, and a ridge of mountainous or rocky elevation, ranging and so parallel with the West-Rock, lies [a] plain, three miles long, containing a thousand or twelve hundred acres of excellent land, which Mr. Goodyear, a rich settler, had bought of the town, and on which he had planted his farmer, Richard Sperry, which farm Richard Sperry afterwards became possessed of, and now for above a century it has gone by the name of Sperry's Farm. In the records I find, April 23, 1660, 'Mrs. Goodyear and her farmer Sperry.' Mr. Goodyear brought farmers with him out of England, being himself an opulent Merchant, and always followed commerce.

"On this tract Mr. Goodyear had built Sperry an house; and in the woods about one mile S. W. from Sperry's, stood the house of Ralph Lines. These were the only two houses in 1661 west ward from New-Haven, between this West Rock and Hudson's River, unless we except a few houses at Derby or Paugasset. All was an immense wilderness. Indeed all the environs of New-Haven was wilderness, except the cleared tract about half a mile or a mile around the town, which was laid out and built with 100 or 120 houses on a square half mile, divided into nine squares. Behind the West Rock therefore was, in 1661, a very secure retreat and concealment. This Mr. Jones provided for these exiles. At and about this mountain they secreted themselves between three and four months. Three harbors, lodgments, or places, of their residence there, at different times, are known and shewn to this day. I have visited all three of them, being carried to and shewn them by the family of the Sperrys still dwelling on that tract.

"At two miles N. W. from the town was a mill. To this mill the judges repaired 11th of May, 1661, and here they lodged two nights. On the 13th, Jones, Burrill and Sperry, came to them in the woods near the south end of the mountain, and conducted them to Sperrys, about three miles from town. They provided for them a place called Hatchet Harbour, where they lay two nights; until a cave or hole in the side of a hill was prepared to conceal them. The hill they called Providence Hill: and there they continued from the 15th of May to the 11th of June ; sometimes in the cave, and in very tempestuous weather in a house near it. [Thus Governor Hutchinson, from Goffe's Journal]."

President Stiles worked very hard at finding the place where the Judges stayed from May 15th to June 11th "In 1785, I visited Mr. Joseph Sperry, then living, aged 76, a grandson of the first Richard, a son of Daniel Sperry, who died 1751, aged 86, from whom Joseph received the whole family tradition. Daniel … built a house at the south end of Sperry's farm, in which Joseph now lives, not half a mile west from the cave, which Joseph shewed me. There is a notch in the mountain against Joseph s house, through which I ascended along a very steep acclivity up to the cave. From the south end of the mountain for three or four miles northward, there is no possible ascent or descent on the west side, but at this notch, so steep is the precipice of the rock. I found the cave to be formed, on a base of perhaps forty feet square, by an irregular clump or pile of rocks, or huge broad pillars of stone, fifteen and twenty feet high, standing erect and elevated above the surrounding superficies of the mountain, and enveloped with trees and forest. These rocks… contiguous at top, furnished hollows or vacuities below, big enough to contain bedding and two or three persons. The apertures being closed with boughs of trees … there might be found a well-covered and convenient lodgment.[17]

"Here [President Stiles continues], Mr. Sperry told me, was the first lodgment of the Judges, and it has ever since gone and been known by the name of the Judges' Cave to this day…. Goffe's Journal says, they entered this Cave the 15th of May, and continued in it till the 11th of June following. Richard Sperry daily supplied them with victuals from his house, about a mile off; sometimes carrying it himself, at other times sending it by one of his boys, tied up in a cloth, ordering him to lay it on a certain stump and leave it: and when the boy went for it at night he always found the basons emptied of the provisions, and brought them home. The boy wondered at it, and used to ask his father the design of it, and he saw no body. His father only told him there was some body at work in the woods that wanted it. The sons always remembered it, and often told it to persons now living, and to Mr. Joseph Sperry particularly."

Why on earth would this be more than a temporary hiding-place? Why would this occur to Sperry (or Burrill or Jones or anyone else) as a hiding-place – given houses and other structures and even apparently better accommodations at Hatchet Harbor? It might have occurred to a man who followed the paths through and about New Haven, particularly if his father did before him, as I think Nicholas Lobdell did. The rocks command a view of the Sound and the country around. Where did Kellond and Kirke go after they left New Haven? They went to the Dutch colony at New Amsterdam. The rocks also command a view of the country to the east and north, where there were problems at this time

---

[17] *Ibid.* pp. 76-77.

with the local "Indians." (Or perhaps the reference to "Indian" problems belongs properly to 1664.)

The answer to this question that Mr. Sperry gave President Stiles should be noted here. "The incident that Mr. Joseph Sperry gave me which broke them up from the Cave was this, that this mountain being a haunt for wild animals, one night as the judges lay in bed, a panther, or catamount, putting his head into the door, or aperture, of the Cave, blazed his eyeballs in such a hideous manner upon them, as greatly affrighted them, One of them was so terrified by this grim and ferocious monster, her eyes and her squalling, that he took to his heels, and fled down the mountain to Sperry's house for safety. They thereupon considered this situation too dangerous, and quitted it. All the Sperry families have this tradition."[18] Whether the tradition is true, exactly, or even in substance, is another question. Judges' Cave, in the year of Our Lord 2013, is entered from the top, which would make a mountain lion at the aperture quite frightening indeed (though not necessarily for experienced soldiers of Oliver Cromwell), but the major difficulty with the story lies in one simple question – how did anyone fleeing get out of the cave past the lion? But that someone fled down the hill from a lion at some time in the memory of the Sperry family is evidently true – which does testify to the presence of lions there, and that could have been a reason for the Judges' removal.

Whether there was any fear of the Dutch at Manhattan is not sure, but they were about to be at war with England (wherein they lost Manhattan in 1664), and relations during Cromwell's Protectorate were not good. (Charles II returned to the Throne of England from the Netherlands and, after all, William of Orange, who became William III

---

[18] *Ibid.* pp. 77-78

of William and Mary, was the son of the Stadtholder William who married the daughter of Charles I and sister of Charles II.) Whether there was any Dutch knowledge involved in choosing the site is likewise not sure – but fragmentary evidence, as I said before, suggests the presence of Nicholas Lobdell or Lobden (1578-1651?) in the area between the Dutch on Manhados and the English at Plymouth as early as 1623. What we have of a canonical record (though more than two centuries afterwards, and obviously subject to the vagaries of folk-memory) has been given above, under the subtitle, "A New-World Scout."

### The Guides, the Pursuivants and the Pursuit

Here's a little of the Report from Kellond and Kirke: "We according to your honor's order departed in search after Colonels Goffe and Whalley (persons declared traitors to his Majesty) from Boston May the 7th, 1661, about six o'clock at night, and arrived at Hartford the 10th day, and repaired to Governor Winthrop, and gave him your honor's letter and his Majesty's order for the apprehending of Colonels Whalley and Goffe, who gave us an account that they did not stay there, but went directly for New-Haven, but informed us that one Symon Lobden guided them to the town."[19] Apart from one or two (important) men in Cambridge (Daniel Gookin and "Captain Pierce"), and one or three on the ship over from England (Daniel Gookin and "Captain Pierce" and William Jones), this Symon Lobden is the first colonist mentioned in connection with hiding Goffe and Whalley. (The tenth day seems a bit long, but then, even this early the older of the Judges could have been nearly seventy.)

---

[19] Stiles, *History*, p. 53

## The Guide for the Judges: Simon Lobdell (1632-1717)

What the Lobdell family knew about Symon Lobden [Simon Lobdell] when gthis inquiry began(besides some family stories whose *locus* was not fully established in their minds) was that he came to Hingham, in Masssachusetts, at the age of three, with his father (Nicholas Lobden or Lobdell), and mother, in 1635. He was born in Northam in Devon, though Nicholas came originally from Eastbourne, in Sussex. Symon was admitted freeman in Milford in 1656. He was a Lieutenant at Springfield before and during King Philip's War, returned to Milford, and eventually seems to have lived with his son Joshua (1671-1743) in Ridgefield (CT), dying there (or perhaps back in Milford) in his 85th year. He was apparently engaged in a pursuit which involved the preparation of hides – possibly from hunting the deer.[20]

It is worth noting that he is the only guide mentioned for Goffe and Whalley, although Kellond and Kirke seem to have had one guide from Boston (Captain Henry Chapin) and another from Hartford (Lieutenant Martin). The author's reconstruction of the career of Nicholas Lobden or Lobdell and its connection with the career of his son Simon, and particularly Simon's involvement here, is still incomplete. Suffice it to say for the present that Nicholas seems to have been a scout and explorer possibly around "Manhados" as early as 1615, and then between "Manhados" and Plymouth Colony in the 1620s, before returning to Devon, marrying, and then returning to the Plymouth outpost at Hingham circa 1635. There are some indications he may have died in 1651.

---

[20] *Records of the Particular Court of Connecticut 1639-1663*, Hartford 1928, p. 175.

Because Simon was a freeman of Milford in 1656, it would seem odd that he was in the Boston/Cambridge area ready to guide Whalley and Goffe to New Haven in 1661, unless perhaps he regularly traveled between Milford and Massachusetts Bay (the geographical area, not the Colony – perhaps to see his father [if still alive] or younger brothers), or unless he had been asked to be there, which would assume an unlikely prior connection between Simon and the Judges. This would be an unlikely – but not an impossible – connection.

Simon's uncle, James Lobdell (also spelled Lopdell), had a son James [1624-1682], Simon's first cousin), who went to Ireland in 1657, there married the daughter or niece of a Sussex neighbor who had earlier entered the Dutch service (John Fennell, with the Dutch *East* India Company), settled near John Whalley, Edward's son, and James Lobdell's son married John Whalley's daughter. That of course happened after 1661, but in 1661 Simon's cousin and Major-General Whalley's son were neighbors in Ireland. Moreover – though this of course is also later on – when Simon's brother John had children in Massachusetts, one of his sons was named Cromwell Lobdell.[21]

One other family connection of interest is that Simon married a woman named Persis (a name common in the Pierce family at the time but not in other families), so that the Persis who married Simon Lobdell was almost certainly connected to the family of the Ferryman of the Atlantic, Captain William Pierce – as the late Father Robbins of New Haven suggested to the author quite a number of years ago. It is worth noting that the will of Thomas Pierce (1665) has substituted the name of Randolph Nicholls (?) for what may be the name of [Nicholas?]

---

[21] J. C. Lobdell, "The Dispersion of the Lobdell/Lopdell Family 1489-1705" in *Sussex Family History* [1977], pp. 81-84.

Lobden[?] erased and read by one Pierce genealogist as "Lowden." Mary Lobdell (1663-1744) married Jonathan Pierce (1661-1722), grandson of Thomas[22]

## The Guides for the Pursuivants: Henry Chapin and Samuel Martin

Henry Chapin [1631-1718], probably then and certainly earlier and later of Springfield, guided Kirke and Kellond from Cambridge to Hartford, and Samuel Martin (emigrated 1645, d. 1683) from Hartford to New Haven. Chapin was in Springfield when Lt. Simon Lobdell was there in and around the time of King Philip's War, and Martin held a Lieutenant's commission in that war. Martin's son William Seaborn Martin, was born at sea in 1653 when his father was returning from a visit to England – and what kind of colonists went back to England in 1652-3? Cromwellian ones, to be sure. Samuel Martin was himself a distinguished resident of the Connecticut shore towns and a Lieutenant in 1677 in King Philip's War, after the great fort-fight. He was designated to bring the Rev. Mr. Cotton from "the Bay" to Wethersfield in 1660, so he had recently been used as a guide for a Puritan minister, not long before Kellond and Kirke.[23]

Henry Chapin lived in Springfield from 1659 till his death in 1718, representing Springfield in the assembly in 1689, and his children continued to live there at least until 1756: family tradition says he was impressed for seven years in the British Navy, was a merchant Captain between London and Boston (either before or after his seven years'

---

[22] W. R. Cutter, *New England Families, Genealogical and Memorial*, Vol. 3 [New York 1914].

[23] T. A. Hay, *Martin Genealogy* [New York 1911], p. 10

service), served during the Anglo-Dutch War of 1652-54, was released, came then to Boston, and shortly to join his father, Deacon Samuel Chapin, in Springfield.[24] (The chronology of his Navy service and merchant service is not entirely clear. Possibly his service was connected with that of the Parliamentary Captain [later Admiral] Nehemiah Bourne of Roxbury 1611-1691. The Chapin family legend about impressment is, in the circumstances, anachronistic.) His body was returned to Paignton, in Devon, after his death in late 1718, and is buried there, next to the grave-marker of his grandfather, lost at sea. He is known as Captain Henry Chapin, the rank being naval, not military. His father, Deacon Samuel Chapin [1598-1675] is the Puritan of Augustus St.- Gauden's statue.

## The Pursuivants: Kellond and Kirke

By their report to Governor Endicott it appears that Kellond and Kirke arrived at New-Haven 13th May 1661; and it would seem that they left the town the next day – though "the constant tradition in New-Haven is, that they diligently searched the town, and particularly the house of Mr. Davenport, whom they treated with asperity and reprehension." Goffe's journal (President Stiles reports) says the Judges left the town the 11th May and went to the Mills, and on the 13th went into the Woods to Sperry's."[25]  Very well – apparently the nights of the 11th and 12th they lodged at the mill (or mills), and on the 13th at Sperry's. Stiles suggests this was so that they might in the day time show themselves at the bridge (at Neck-Rock, now East-Rock) when the pursuers passed it, and

---

[24] Orange Chapin, *The Chapin Genealogy* [Northampton 1862], pp. 5-6

[25] Stiles, *History*, p. 61

possibly at Mrs. Eyers's in town the same or next day, in order to clear Mr. Davenport of his having concealed them, and return at night to their concealment – all of which, at this distance in time, seems over-complicated and unlikely: but they may have been at Mrs. Eyers's – Captain Allerton's – after leaving the cave.)

The Sperry family, Stiles remarks, "are uniform in the family tradition that the surprisal of the Judges at their ancestor's house" was by the pursuers from England, Kellond and Kirke, "known and distinguishable, as they said, from our own people by their red coats" – but this "surprisal," Stiles goes on to say, could not have been by Kellond and Kirke, as they stayed in town but one day. As to that one day, President Stiles argues that, "on the one hand, it is improbable they would spend but one day in a town where they did not doubt the regicides … were; and on the other hand, 'tis doubtful whether they would do much at actual searching themselves without the Governor's warrant, which was refused."[26] As to the fact of a "surprisal" at all – the evidence is at best mixed (and a century after). As to the red coats – they are (to me) so anachronistic and improbable that they cast doubt on much of the rest of this part of the story. As to the "zealous Royalists" Kellond and Kirke – well, it's time for a re-examination of the evidence. Who were Thomas Kellond and Thomas Kirke?

We have two incontrovertible and acknowledged facts about Thomas Kellond – we don't know for sure when he was born (1636? 1638?) or when he died (1683? 1686?) – we know his will, dated 1683, left an estate of £4884, more than was left by Governor William Phips, and we know he was the uncle of the Governor Hutchinson who

---

[26] Stiles, *History*, p. 63

collected the available documentary materials on Goffe and Whalley in pre-Revolutionary Massachusetts, with a strong motive to play down any activities of his kin against the Crown.[27]

We also know Kellond married into several good Boston Puritan families, was rich, traded along the Atlantic coast and perhaps to the Caribbean, was chosen Constable in Boston in 1673, and were it not for his nephew's possibly self-serving statement that he was a Royalist, one would have trouble deducing it from his actions. (As a matter of some interest, there is, in Westchester County [NY], record of an Indenture between John Foster of Boston, Esq., and Abigail his wife, late the relict and widow of Thomas Kellond of Boston, Merchant, on the one hand, and Samuel Palmer of Mamaroneck, January 13, 1701.[28]

Of Thomas Kirke we know less. Even the statement that he was a ship's captain or sea-captain may be suspect, and one identification of him as related to the three British heroes of the capture of Quebec in 1629[29] – Captains (or Admirals) David Kirke, Lewis Kirke, and Thomas Kirke – makes this clear.[30] James Savage, in his great *Genealogical Dictionary*, says about him only what is in Hutchinson and Stiles. He does not seem to have remained in Boston – but then, as a ship's captain,

---

[27] A. L. Cummings, "The Foster-Hutchinson House" in *Old-Time New England*, Vol. LIV [1964], pp. 59-61.

[28] *N.Y. Genealogical and Biographical Record*, Vol. 51 [1920], p. 253.

[29] *Collections of the Massachusetts Historical Society*, Vol. XXVII [1836], p. 128.

[30] Henry Fitzgilbert Waters, *Genealogical Gleanings in England*, Volume 2 [Boston 1901 and Salem 1907 reprinted Baltimore 1969]. James Savage, *Genealogical Dictionary of the First Settlers of New England* [Cambridge MA 1860].

he might not. If he were connected with the brothers Kirke, it should be remembered that five-sixths of their Newfoundland grant went to Oliver Cromwell's son-in-law Claypoole.[31]

But even if he were connected to the brothers (and he was certainly not one of them), what happened to him after 1661? There is a Thomas Kirke in Boston ca. 1686 but he is a cobbler. There is a Thomas Kirke in Maine, but it is difficult to find out much about him and not at all clear that he was a sea-captain. There is a Thomas Kirke with lands in Virginia circa 1658 – but this Thomas Kirke died in 1665, and it was he who was said to be one of the brothers.[32] And there was a Thomas Kirke who married in 1657, in England, one Judith Pell, daughter of Dr. John Pell (1611-1685), brother of Thomas Pell (d. 1669), who married a Brewster of New-Haven, first Lord of the Manor of Pelham – and thus Judith was the sister and this Thomas Kirke the brother-in-law of Sir John Pell (1643-1702), second Lord of the Manor of Pelham.[33]

Dr. John Pell (1611-1685) was Cromwell's Minister to the Protestant Cantons of Switzerland in 1654-58, when this Thomas Kirke married his daughter. This Thomas Kirke is found living in Pelham in

---

[31] *Dictionary of Canadian Biography* [on-line] s.n. Kirke, David (1597-1654), shows the Kirkes originally as Royal servants, then compounding during the Civil War (and giving five-sixths of their Newfoundland lands to Claypoole, for whatever reason) – then having the lands they disputed with Lord Calvert awarded to [the Catholic] Calvert by [the Catholic?] Charles II.

[32] See Nell M. Nugent, *Cavaliers and Pioneers: Abstracts of Virginia Land Patents and Grants 1623-1666* [Richmond 1934].

[33] T. G. Bergen, *Genealogies of the State of New York*, Volume 1 [New York 1915], p. 235

1684, when he witnessed the will of one Nathaniel Tompkins; his grandson Thomas is a mariner there circa 1740, and it will be remembered that Pelham has been described in these words: "The manor was famous for its location near to the great seaport; its fishing in the vicinity was unsurpassed the entire length of the sound" – quite a reasonable place for a ship-captain.[34]  Thomas C. Kirke, Sr., was a Grand Juryman there in 1687, which I take to be about the time he died.

If this is our Thomas Kirke, he was a Cromwellian, not a Royalist, and if he was kin to the brothers Kirke (who by the way were Huguenots), it was not as one of the brothers, though it is possible he could have been a son. The legend of his connection with the heroes of Quebec in 1629 seems to be contemporary, and the heroes of Quebec certainly had connections with at least one member of Cromwell's family, albeit having been loyal servants of King Charles before the days of his personal rule. What is more important than 1629here is 1661 and thereafter.

### The Searchers from Milford: Tapping, Campe, Sanford, Ward

Here we may insert a Milford document, relating to the search that began May 14th 1661.[35] "By order of the General Court, Jasper Crane, as attest, Matthew Gilberte, William Leete, Deputie Governour. Robert Treatt. In the Marshalls absence, I doe appoint and impower you,

---

[34] Robert Bolton, *History of the Several Towns, Manors, and Patents of the County of Westchester* [2nd edition, New York 1881], II, s.n. 'Pelham' [pp. 27-99].

[35] Charles Hoadly, *Records from the Colony or Jurisdiction of New Haven, from May 1653 to the Union* [Hartford 1858], pp, 389ff.

Thomas Sanford, Nicholas Campe, and James Tapping to the above named powers, according to the tenour of the warrant; and to make a returne thereof under your hands to me by the first. Robert Treatt." And their sworn response, dated May 20th: "Wee, the said persons, appointed to serve and search by virtue of this our warrant, doe hereby declare and testifie that to our best light we have the 20th of May, 1661, made diligent search according to the tenour of this warrant, as witness our hands. Thomas Sanford, Nicholas Campe, James Tapping, Lawrence Ward, his mark" (the mark rather than a signature suggests the cobbler Lawrence Ward Sr. rather than the Deacon, Lawrence Ward Jr.). This search coincided with the beginning of the Judges' time in the "Cave" on West Rock.

Of Thomas Sanford (1608?-1681) we know a fair amount. He came to New England (on the *Arabella*, according to Banks; to Boston in 1631, according to Holmes) with several brothers, following their uncle Andrew Warner, and may have been at Dorchester as early as 1632. He lived in Dorchester at least from 1634 to 1640 then moved to Milford [CT] where he was admitted to the church on January 9, 1641/2. His wife, Sarah, was admitted to the Milford church on December 15, 1642. His will dated September 23, 1681 (estate inventoried October 21st) mentions eldest son Ezekiel, sons Thomas, Ephraim, Samuel; daughters Sarah (wife of Richard Shute of Eastchester), Elizabeth (wife of Obadiah Allyn of Middletown); grandchildren Sarah Shute and Thomas Allyn; and maid Sarah Whitlock.[36]

---

[36] C. E. Banks, *Topographical Dictionary of 2885 English Emigrants to New England 1620-1650* [1937, reprinted Baltimore 2007]; Carlton Sanford, *Thomas Sanford, the Emigrant to New England* [Rutland VT 1911]; W. R. Cutter, *New England Families, Genealogical and Memorial*, Vol. 3 [New York 1914].

Nicholas Campe may be Nicholas Junior (1627-1706), who came with his parents Nicholas (1606-1662) and Sarah (Elliott) Campe (1599-1645) to America, or he may be Nicholas Senior. Nicholas (Jr.) married 14 Jul 1652 (probably in Milford), Sarah Beard, daughter of the widow Martha Beard, whose husband, James Beard, probably died on the ship *Martin* on its voyage to America.[37] Nicholas started a store on the west end of Milford – the area also where Simon Lobdell settled (or at least had his house lot) -- and over the years became a successful businessman.[38] This Nicholas (Jr.) and Sarah were the parents of eight known children including Mary Camp (b. 1660), who married one Joseph Peck, whose family later intermarried with that of Simon Lobdell. After the death of his Sarah, this Nicholas married (2) Mehitabel, the widow of Nathaniel Briscoe.

James Topping (or Tapping or Tappin or Toppin) was probably the James Topping (dying apparently in 1712, but possibly on Long Island in 1694) who married Hannah Garrett, March 5th 1656, in Milford or Guilford or Middletown[39] and it would not be amiss to think that he and Nicholas Campe the younger and Simon Lobdell might have been connected in business. They seem in any case to have been of an age:

---

[37] R. N. and C. C. Mann, *Camp-Kemp Family History* [Cedar Bluffs AL 1967]; Banks, *Topographical Dictionary*; Cutter, *New England Families*.

[38] *Public Records of the Colony of Connecticut*, Vol. 3, p. 452: "In letter by Tho: Trowbridge to Gov. Andros dated Aug., 8, 1688 regarding a Justice from Milford. He writes "and there is one Mr. Campe of Milford, a man of good estate and many with us doe thinke him a fitt person, but leave it to yo'r Excelency's discretion."

[39] *New England Marriages before 1700*, p. 727; G. R. Howell, *Early History of Southampton, L.I.* [New York 1887].

whether this is the James Tapping who was baptized in 1643 seems a little unlikely, though Tapping family tradition asserts the identity of this James with the Milford searcher: Long Island tradition, on the other hand, places the birth of James Topping in Bedfordshire in 1632 (the same year Simon Lobdell was born in Devon). The Long Island tradition seems to fit in better with other data.

Lawrence Ward (who is probably Lawrence Ward Sr., the ship's carpenter Lawrence Ward, rather than Lawrence Ward the younger, the Deacon) may be the Lawrence Ward who died in Newark in 1670. In any case, Lawrence Ward Sr. was involved in the building of New Haven's Lost Ship. Whether senior or junior, Nicholas Campe and Lawrence Ward were, like Sanford (of the older generation) and Tapping (presumably of the younger) sectarians of the New Haven/Newark sort – and it would be almost a foregone conclusion that they (or any connected with them) would not find the fugitives their colleagues and friends were hiding.[40]

---

[40] On the two Lawrence Wards, see Cutter, *New England Families*, Vol. 1 [New York 1914]; on Lawrence Ward the younger, see materials on the founding of Newark NJ [1666] where he is an original landowner; and on the family see Isabel M. Calder, *The New Haven Colony* [New Haven 1934]; also Banks, *Topographical Dictionary*; R. R. Hinman, *A Catalogue of the Names of the Early Puritan Settlers of the Colony of Connecticut* [Hartford 1852]

## Interlude, Second Hiding, and the Aftermath

So they came out of the Cave on June 11<sup>th</sup>, and they went to Milford for their several years' sojourn there somewhat later. Then they were in Milford till (it was said) October 1664, and then north to Hadley, where Whalley died and Goffe may have. Except for the appearance of the "Angel of Hadley" (perhaps Goffe – certainly one of the two) in King Philip's War, we pretty much lose sight of them when they left Milford for Hadley to the north – though it is true we have aq rec9ord that they stopped at a Pilgrim's Harbor on the way.

### Interlude 1661: The Grand Houses and especially "Mrs. Eyers's"

By "Interlude" we mean the time between the Judges' leaving their cave and their beginning their final (or at least three-year) hiding in Milford. At some point after June 11<sup>th</sup> the Judges went to Milford, to the home of Micah Tompkins, but in the meantime they seem to have at one of the "grand houses" in New Haven, presumably that of Mrs. Eyers (meaning that of Captain Isaac Allerton). Here is President Stiles, again seeking history from traditional stories.[41] "Mrs. Sherman, relict of Mr. James Sherman, aged 86, a descendant from Governor Leete, whose daughter married a Trowbridge, from whom Mrs. Sherman. She tells me she was born in Governor Jones's or in Governor Eaton's house [that is, the house once owned by Eaton, then by his son-in-law Jones], which had nineteen fire-places, and many apartments; where Goffe and Whalley used to reside; that Mr. Davenport's house also had many apartments, and thirteen fire-places, which … I myself well remember, having frequently, when a boy, been all over the house.

---

[41] *History*, pp. 63-64.

'She was intimately acquainted with Mrs. Eyers, and is full of the story of the Judges being secreted at her house, which was repeatedly searched for them." President Stiles goes on to suggest "that this house was twice searched, and the circumstances are a little blended in the different narratives. The first was by the pursuers, when the Judges went out at the back door, and returned and were secreted in the closet while the pursuers were in the house. The other was immediately after the pursuers left the town, and between the 14th and 17th of May [the search by Sanford, Campe, Tapping, and Ward], when the search was made by Governor Leete's orders, when the doors were all set open, and Mrs. Eyers [actually, one supposes, her parent or parents] left the house for the searchers to come in and examine every room: this was by our people [Sanford, Campe, Tapping, and Ward] ...

"Mrs. Sherman considers and speaks of the search not as once only, but at several or different times.[42] She says Mrs. Eyers had on one side of the room a large wainscotted closet, which she has often viewed and admired: it had cut lights at top, full of pewter and brass, and a wainscot door, which, when shut, could not be distinguished from the wainscot, and all over the door, and on the outside of the closet, was hung braizery and elegant kitchen furniture, that no one would think of entering the closet on that breast-work. Here she hid the Judges.—It seems to her as is it was more than once.—That they used to frequent the house on Saturdays afternoon, when sometimes she shut them up, and then opened all the doors, and walked abroad, leaving all open for the pursuers to search." (How much veridical content we have here is decidedly uncertain.)

---

[42] Stiles, *History*, pp. 66ff

Mrs. Sherman adds that "Mrs. Eyers's father was Mr. Isaac Allerton, of Boston, a sea Captain, who came early and settled in New-Haven, and built a grand house on the creek with four porches, and this with Governor Eaton's, Mr. Davenport's, and Mr. Gregson's, were the grandest houses in town [this confuses Captain Isaac Allerton of Plymouth, Pierce's associate, with his son, Mrs. Eyers's father]. The house highly finished: he had a fine garden with all sorts of flowers, and fruit-trees, and in the best cultivation. Mr. Eyers was also a sea Captain, pursuing foreign voyages up the Mediterranean and to the wine islands, and always had his cellar stored with wines and good liquors, and used to bring home much produce and foreign manufactures, and elegant Nuns' work. Both went long voyages, and both died abroad at sea near together, leaving her a young widow – who never married again. She possessed her father's, brother's and husband's estates" (but not in 1661 when she was eight years old, and the house was her late grandfather's). And then we learn that "Captain Willmot, aged 82, remembers the story of their being hid in Mrs. Eyers's house when the pursuers came there. He remembers the old house; that it was grand, like Mr. Davenport's, which he also knew, and all of oak and the best of joiner's work. There was more work and better Joiner- work in these houses, he says, than in any house now in town. He is a joiner, and helped to pull down Mrs. Eyers's house."

## The Hiding in Milford 1661-1664

The second hiding comes with the Judges in their "Ebenezer" in Milford, in 1661-1664, going back to their Cave for a short time, then – which is the third hiding, which we cover as the "Aftermath" – we have their walking the eighty-five miles through Hartford and Springfield to Hadley, and what happened there. But why to Milford, and where in

Milford? The story is told, of course, by President Stiles, and it answers our second query first.[43]

"From their lodgments in the woods [in 1664], the Judges removed and took asylum in the house of Mr. Tompkins, in the centre of Milford, thirty or forty rods from the meeting-house. Governor Law afterwards bought this house and lot, and built his seat within a rod or two of it I have frequently been in this house of Tomkins's, in the Governor's lifetime, who died 1750, aged 73; it was standing since 1750 and perhaps to 1770. In this house the two Judges resided in most absolute concealment, not so much as walking out into the orchard for two years. I have not learned who were privy to the concealment here. The minister at this time was the Rev. Roger Newton. He with Mr. Treat and Mr. Fenn and a few others were in the secret, and held interviews with them in their secret retirement. But it is strange that the very memory of their residence there is almost totally obliterated. I do not find a single person of Milford, or of Milford extract, except Judge Law, … the governor's son , and Gideon Buckingham, Esq. of Milford, now living, who is possessed of any idea or tradition of the Judges having ever lived there at all."

From Judge Law came the information that their house "was built for the Judges on Tomkins's lot, a few rods from his house. It was a building, say twenty feet square, and two stories, the lower room built with stone wall and considered as a store, the room over it with timber and wood, and used by Tomkins's family as a work or spinning room. The family used to spin in the room above, ignorant of the Judges being below, where they resided two years without going abroad so much as

---

[43] Stiles, *History*, pp.88-89.

into the orchard."[44]    Judge Buckingham told him "this story, the only anecdote or notice I could ever learn from, a Milford man now living. While they were sojourning in Milford, there came over from England a lascivious Cavalier ballad, satirizing Charles's Judges, and Goffe and Whalley among the rest. A spinstress in Milford had learned to sing it, and used sometimes to sing it in the chamber over the Judges; and the Judges used to get Tompkins to set the girls to singing that song, for their diversion. Being humoured and pleased with it, though at their own expense, as they were the subjects of the ridicule. The girls knew nothing of the matter, being ignorant of the innocent device, and little thought that they were serenading angels."[45]

This tells us pretty much *where*, along with giving a kind of sidelight on Goffe and Whalley, but it does not tell us *why* the move to Milford. Perhaps what President Stiles says of the move from Milford may give a hint. "Afterwards [that is, after living in the store-house cellar] their religious meetings and exercises, it is said, gave them too much notoriety to continue there any longer, and they were obliged to meditate move to a more secreted asylum. This was undoubtedly accelerated by the news of the arrival of the Commissioners at Boston, 1664, one of whose instructions from the king was to make enquiry for Colonel Whalley and Colonel Goffe. They sought for the most remote frontier settlement, and their friends provided for their reception at the house of the Rev. John Russel, minister of the new-settled town of Hadley, one hundred miles off, upon Connecticut River, in

---

[44] Stiles, *History*, p.89

[45] Stiles, *History*, pp. 89-90

Massachusetts. They removed from Milford to Hadley upon the 13$^{th}$ of October 1664."[46]

So why to Milford? That was, apparently, where Simon Lobdell ("of Milford 1656") had first taken them – and then they had returned to New Haven, closer to their protectors (John Davenport or William Leete, perhaps), or for some other reason. But then, for whatever reason, catamounts (less likely) or "Indians" (more likely), they had left New Haven and returned to Milford. Or perhaps their time in New Haven was simply to enable their "Ebenezer" to be built – as a storehouse – while they were away from public view in Milford. After all, they left Milford, it is said, when it became too widely known that they were there – though the coincidence with the English capture of New Amsterdam is suggestive.

Simon Lobdell was a leading "afterplanter" of Milford (listed as 1646, possibly because he held land purchased by 1645, but more correctly he would be 1656), while Micah Tompkins was an original [1639] planter (Lot 15 in the center of town).[47] If Simon's property was part of the 1655 purchase, it was it was in the region between Paugusset [Derby] and the Two-Mile Path – in other words, north of Milford, though he also held property in the west of Milford. In his will his house-lot adjoins that of Walter Smith. There is no proof that Micah Tompkins [1615-1690] and the younger Simon Lobdell [1632-1717], were neighbors in Milford. But a store-house has to have something to store, even if it is also a cover for storing Goffe and Whalley, and perhaps this one stored hides or leather, from Simon Lobdell.

---

[46] Stiles, *History*, p. 97.

[47] Julia Harrison Lobdell, *Simon Lobdell of Milford CT 1646* [Chicago 1907], p. 4

## The Aftermath 1664-?

And why from Milford? And how did they go? There is no mention of a guide. Here is what President Stiles has to say:[48] "On the 13th of October 1664 they left Milford, and proceeded in this excursion. In shall suppose that the first night they came over to their friend Jones, though of this there is no tradition, as there is of their making a lodgment at Pilgrim's Harbor, so called from them, being twenty miles from New Haven, at a place called Meriden, half way between New Haven and Hartford. Here they might rest and lodge one day, and the next proceed to Hartford, and the night following to Springfield, and the succeeding night reach Hadley. But of this I find no tradition, saving only that in their route to Hadley, they made one station at Pilgrim's Harbor." (In fact, "Pilgrim's Harbor" was so called before the Judges stayed there[49] – though curiously a similarly named refuge in Meriden in old England had sheltered the Rev. John Davenport and others: but the minister who had provided that refuge in England went to Guilford in 1638, not Milford. We may need to find a family connection with Meriden in 1664 amongst our families in New Haven Colony.)

So much (a little) for the *how?* What of the *why?* Possibly, as suggested above, because of the British capture of Manhados and the new "ownership" of New England by James, Duke of York, later (as James II) the last Roman Catholic monarch of England. Possibly because of 'Indian" troubles. But quite likely (at least as a contributing cause) from the impending break-up of the Cromwellian nucleus at

---

[48] Stiles, *History*, p. 108.

[49] C. B. Gillespie, *Historic Record and Pictorial Description of the Town of Meriden* [Meriden 1907], pp. 37, 46.

Milford – Simon Lobdell to Springfield, Micah Tompkins to Newark, and so on (both these in 1666), after the loss of the New Haven charter. In any case, the Judges went to Hadley. The final appearance – one might say the *encore finale* – is well-known, but not indisputable. It is at Hadley, Massachusetts, during King Philip's War (date disputed but most likely 1676), and it is the story of the Angel of Hadley. It need not be re-told here, except insofar as a re-telling may suggest an alternative to the generally accepted form of the story. The suggestion here is that Whalley was Goffe's senior by about a dozen years, perhaps more, rather than two years his junior (which would make him ten when his daughter was born)., that he was not seen, certainly not after his mind was damaged by his stroke in 1675, but Goffe as Goldsmith had drilled the troops, and a sudden apparition was more likely Whalley.

In this connection, Walter Scott in his *Peveril of the Peak* fundamentally attributes the legend of the "Angel of Hadley" – the ancient soldier who appeared unexpectedly to save the town of Hadley (MA) in King Philip's War – to Whalley rather than Goffe, and it seems probable (in disagreement with most scholars) that Sir Walter is right. Goffe was well-known in the settlement as Walter Goldsmith and had indeed drilled the troops in archery: he was a healthy man of perhaps threescore and ten ("and some be so strong they reach fourscore years"), while by our calculation Whalley was in his eighties. He died not long after – but it may be that Goffe did not die in 1679. The persistent rumor that one of the Regicides (presumably Goffe) died about the same time as John Dixwell, the third Regicide in New Haven, around 1689, and was secretly buried in Dixwell's grave, suggests he lived another ten years (even if buried elsewhere).

What was he like, this William Goffe? He had been brought up, it is said, as a salter's boy in London; and he told tales of tumults in the

London streets, which he had greatly liked, so much so that he went for a soldier and forgot his trade.[50] And it was said of him afterwards that he so much liked the fighting he forgot for what he fought (but in his exile he was forever seeking comfort in Holy Writ). One of his brothers was a clergyman of the Established Church, and another of them was what William Goffe would call a Papist priest to the French Queen of England. And what was Edward Whalley like? Even in 1661 he must have been near three-score years and ten (or even more): his famous scene (if it is his) comes more than a decade after he and Goffe went to Hadley. For what it is worth, here is a reconstruction of that event (based in part on family tradition). For those who cannot accept the accuracy of such a family tradition, we could call it imaginative or creative non-fiction. We will take it here, *arguendo*, as the truth. (The story is told by Cooper and Hawthorne and Walter Scott, among others – some make Goffe the "Angel of Hadley" but Scott makes it Whalley, and that seems the more probable.) Here is our story (remember, this has no *independent* evidentiary value):

"The men and the boys of Hadley took their places, as the Colonel had planned, who had drilled them, and they were repelling the attack, though with difficulty, for the Indians were many and the blood of their young men was up. The firing of the guns brought the old General to the street, where he had not been these ten years and more. His garments had been old-fashioned in the London of 1640, for he kept to the clothes of his youth and there he stood in doublet and hose, his white hair standing up, ringed about his head, for he was hatless. 'Willie!' he called, 'Who is it comes with drum and musket to disturb my peace?' And the Colonel, his son-in-law, answers, 'It is Philip's men.'

---

[50] Stiles, *History*, pp. 10ff.

"Then the old General cries out, 'What, King Philip comes?' And when the Colonel answers 'Ay,' he mutters, 'Then are the Spanish fighting for the Man of Blood?' and draws his sword of Naseby Field, and cries out in a great cry 'Up, musketeers! and at 'em, in God's name!' And he is himself up and over the palisado, the Colonel following the General to keep him from harm, the men and boys following the Colonel to the attack, and the Indians thinking that a *manito* from the past has come to lead the settlers. They flee in haste from the spirit. The Colonel gets his General back to Minister Russell's nor is he ever seen again by living man beyond the house, nor is it thought he lived long thereafter."

Whenever made and by whom (in our family), it is clearly a reconstruction, unless it is a tale so oft-repeated that the words have become a formula – and the former is much more likely. But then, all the accounts of the "Angel of Hadley" are reminiscent and to some degree reconstructions.

## Family Ties and Atlantic Citizens

The family ties of the pursuivants (and their Milford colleagues) have already suggested that the pursuit was not entirely designed to catch the pursued, as well as indicating the strength of Cromwellian connections in New England. But looking at family ties can also tell us about cross-Atlantic links in a Commonwealth of the North Atlantic. We already know that one of the guides for the pursuivants was a merchant captain and veteran of the British Navy, presumably under Robert Blake [1598-1657] – whether under Nehemiah Bourne [1611-1691] of Boston and Charlestown and Dorchester, Admiral under Blake, cannot be said. But, like Nehemiah Bourne, his life was on both sides of the Atlantic, like Daniel Gookin and William Pierce, considered above.

### Hiders: Davenport, Jones, Burril, Sperry, Meigs, Eyers, Scranton

John Davenport's life is pretty well-known, but it will do no harm to rehearse parts of it here. Davenport (April 9, 1597 – May 30, 1670) was born in Coventry, Warwickshire, to a wealthy family. He was educated at Oxford University, matriculating at Merton College in 1613 but migrating to Magdalen College two years later, eventually leaving Oxford before completing his degree. His father was Henry Davenport (d. May 29, 1627), draper, alderman, and Mayor of Coventry, son of Edward Davenport, Mayor of Coventry (1551), and Margery Harford. His mother, Winifred Barnaby (1569 - April 12, 1597), was most probably a descendant of William I of Scotland and of Henry I of England and a direct descendant of an illegitimate son of Henry II and Rosamond de Clifford. After serving as the chaplain of Hilton Castle he became the minister of St. Stephen Coleman Street in London. In 1625 he returned to Oxford for further studies. Following a disagreement over the inclusion of the destitute in church congregations, in 1633 he resigned from the established church and moved to Holland.[51]

While in Holland, it was believed that he was the model for several portraits by Rembrandt, now thought to be self-portraits of Rembrandt. In 1637 he acquired the patent for a colony in Massachusetts and sailed with much of his congregation for Boston. In March 1638 he co-founded the Colony of New Haven along with his classmate, Theophilus Eaton, the wealthy London merchant who became the colony's first governor. As burgess, he was a doubly important figure in the colony until he left for Boston in 1669. He died there of apoplexy in 1670 and was buried in the same tomb as John Cotton in King's Chapel Burying Ground.

William Jones has been said (see, e.g., Wilson, p. 525) to have been the son of the Regicide *John Jones* and *Catherine Cromwell*, but this is virtually certainly untrue. He was born 1624 in London, long before John Jones married Catherine, and there is no evidence whatever that he was at all related to any John Jones (not an uncommon name). He died 17 Oct 1706 in New Haven, having been elected Lt. Gov. of New Haven Colony 25 May 1664, a Commissioner of the United Colonies, Magistrate of the Union of New Haven and Connecticut Colonies in 1665, and eventually, July 9, 1691, Lt. Governor (effectively Governor) of Connecticut. He married Hannah Eaton on July 7, 1659, in St Andrews Church, Westminster, London, she being the daughter of Theophilus Eaton (the New Haven founder and first Governor) and Anne Lloyd.[52]

---

[51] Francis J. Bremer, *John Davenport: A Puritan in Three Worlds* [New Haven: Yale 2012]

[52] Judith McGhan, *Genealogies of Connecticut Families* from the *New England Historical and Genealogical Review* Volume II [Baltimore 1983]

What is curious about the account of hiding the Judges in the Cave is that William Jones is credited with taking the Judges there – but he had been in the colony only a short time and on the other side of New Haven. It is true Sperry lived near the cave and supplied food, but how did he come to be involved? Perhaps the answer lies with the third man mentioned. John Burwell came to America from Hemel Hempstead, Hertfordshire, and was made a Free Planter, settled in Wepawaug (now Milford) 1639, but from his dying so early (Aug. 17, 1649), Milford records do not contain much information concerning him. He had five sons and a daughter Elizabeth: (1) John, *b.* in England; (2) Zarachiah, *b.* in England; (3) Samuel, *b.* 1640; (4) Ephraim, *b.* 19th May, 1644; (5) Nathan, *b.* 1646; (6) Elizabeth, *b.* 1647. Samuel Burwell (Lieut.), son of John Burwell and Alice, was b. Oct. 11, 1640 (d. May 5, 1715); his daughter Mary (b. October 20th 1667) married Joshua Lobdell, son of Simon. (The marriage was performed by Governor Robert Treat.)

Which Burwell or Burrill appears in the *History* is uncertain – Samuel would have been 21, John Jr. older. Our suggestion here is that, whichever it was, the Burwell in question, like John Meigs and Simon Lobdell, was a "pathman" – a hunter and scout, principally to the north and east of New Haven, but west and south as far as Milford.[53]

Richard Sperry was born in February 16, 1606 in Thurleigh, Bedfordshire. He died 1693/96 in New Haven, married in 1648 in New Haven to Dennis (Dionys) Goodyear (1627-1707). He arrived on June 26th, 1637, in Boston at the Massachusetts Bay Colony, on the ship *Hector.* His group of colonists was headed by Reverend John Davenport

---

[53] Susan Woodruff Abbott, *Families of Early Milford Connecticut* [Baltimore 1979]

and Theophilus Eaton (who later became the Governor). Several published accounts show Richard coming to America as an agent of or being sent by the Earl of Warwick. It is certain that he was gardener/farmer for Deputy Governor Stephen Goodyear who was an agent of the Earl of Warwick. This was presumably Sir Robert Rich, second earl of Warwick, who in 1631 was granted the patent for colonizing in Connecticut. An early land record dated January 4th 1643 shows Sperry was granted a large tract of land, the tenure of ownership on which, according to a paper on the Sperry family by Rodney Homer in 1969, was upwards of 250 years. Another record dated the same day shows him being fined in New Haven Colony "for having a defect in his gun cock". He was granted free colony fellowship as a "freeman" July 1st, 1644. According to *Historic Woodbridge*, in 1648 Richard Sperry was the first settler in Woodridge and built the first home on the west side of Amity Road.[54]

John Meigs, on the other hand, was a Guilford – indeed a Hammonasset – man. There may be some question whether John Meigs Sr., or Jr. is being referred to. As a rider in 1661 it might have been John Jr. (b. 1641), but the John Meigs who was a pathman (if he was) most likely was John Sr. (1612-1672). At one point this John Meigs was a tanner and currier (he sued a shoemaker named Gregory in New Haven in 1647 for the unworkmanlike manner in which several pairs of shoes had been cut). (Simon Lobdell seems also to have been connected with the trade in leather – hides, at least – which might well be a concomitant for being a frontier pathman, as John Meigs Sr. presumably was). In 1657 one John Meigs (possibly the younger) was reprimanded for

---

[54] *Historic Woodbridge: An Historic and Architectural Resource Survey* [Woodbridge CT 1994]

making too much noise coming with his cart from Hammonasset on the Sabbath. On the other hand, in the will of John Meigs the elder (1671), described as of the new plantation of Hammonnassett, he left his son John a notable selection of books and manuscripts. He was son of the immigrant Vincent Meigs (1583-1658), and once (1648-1658) owned the lot at the corner of Church and Chapel streets in New Haven.[55]

To look at Mrs. Eyers (remembering that she was there when the Judges were hidden, but was a child of eight), we must first look at Isaac Allerton Sr. (associate of Pierce the Ferryman). Isaac Allerton Sr (her grandfather) was b. ca. 1586 d. 1658 New Haven, Connecticut married 1st Mary Norris, granddaughter of Sir Henry Norris. [John Norris who came to Virginia on the *Truelove* in 1635 was the son of Sir Henry Norris]. He married 2nd Fear Brewster, daughter of William Brewster of Plymouth Colony. He married 3rd Joanna Swinnerton (no children). By Mary Norris Allerton had children (1) Bartholomew Allerton, b. 1612 Leyden, Holland; (2) Remember Allerton, b. 1614 Leyden, Holland, died 1656, married Moses Maverick about 1635. He was of Devon County England, and died at Marblehead, MA; (3). Mary Allerton, b. 1616 Leyden, Holland, died 1699 Plymouth, the last survivor of those who came of the *Mayflower*. She married Thomas Cushman; (4) child buried at St Peter, Leyden in 1620; (5) stillborn son born Plymouth Harbor on the Mayflower Dec 22, 1620. Mary died two months later.[56]

[55]B. C. Steiner, *History of Guilford and Madison CT* (1897 reprinted Guilford 1975) p. 129.

[56] Barbara Lambert Merrick, "Important Allerton-Brewster Connections" in *Mayflower Descendant*, Vol. 42 [1992], pp. 117ff, and see Waters, *Genealogical Gleanings*, and Savage, *Genealogical Dictionary*.

His children by Fear Brewster Allerton (daughter of William Brewster) included (6) Sarah Allerton b. 1627, died 1651, and (7) Isaac Allerton, Jr., born ca. 1628 at Plymouth Colony, died 1702 Westmoreland Co., VA. He graduated from Harvard in 1650. He married 1st Elizabeth [last name unknown] and she died sometime after the birth of their first child. The child was Elizabeth (our Mrs. Eyers, but of course the grand house must have been the Allerton house). Elizabeth Allerton Eyers was born at New Haven in 1653 and died at New Haven circa 1740 (mother of six children) married, first. Benjamin Starr, and then married, second, Simon Ayers/Eyers, by whose name she is known.

Dennis Crampton, or Scranton, of Guilford in 1656, probably as a bound apprentice, born in Kent [England] 1636, married on 16 Sept. 1660, Mary, daughter of John Parmelee – so was newly married at our time – and had Hannah, Elizabeth, and Nathaniel, this last born March 1667, and Mary died on the 16th of the same month. By his second wife Sarah, widow of Nicholas Munger, he had children Sarah, born 17 December 1669; Thomas, 25 November 1672; and John, 16 June 1675. He lived some years at Killingworth, but went back to Guilford before his marriage to his third wife Frances, was living there 1685; and died 31 January 1690, leaving a good estate. This much we know about him, but we do not know certainly the original form of his name, though it seems his descendants are called Scranton, not Crampton.[57]

### The Special Case: Micah Tompkins

Micah Tompkins was the son of Ralph Tompkins and Katherine Foster. He married Mary Pennington on 12 December 1643, and died in

---

[57] Alvan Talcott, *Families of Early Guilford Connecticut* [Baltimore 1984].

1690 at Newark (East Jersey), being one of Davenport's settlers in 1666-67. His will was probated December 4th 1690 at Newark. He was christened in 1615 in Buckingham. The first reference in American genealogical records to Micah Tompkins speaks of his removal with his wife, Mary, in 1639, from Wethersfield, Conn., to the site of the present town of Milford, Conn., purchased August 28, 1639 from the Indian chief, Ausautawae. As a list of settlers in Wethersfield from 1635 to 1660 does not contain the name of Micah Tompkins, he may have remained at Wethersfield but a short time. Careful investigation has shown that Micah Tompkins did not originally land or subsequently reside at Plymouth, Salem, or Watertown, Mass. On page 1 of Book I of the town records of Milford there is entered a list of the freemen of that town, dated November 20, 1639, which includes the name of Micah Tompkins.[58]  Bolton in his *History of Westchester County,* says that Micah Tompkins, of Milford, Conn., was of the same family as John Tompkins of Concord (1640), progenitor of the Tompkins family of Pelham.

As one of the first settlers of Milford, Micah Tompkins had set off to him, out of the first subdivision of town sites, a house lot (No. 15) of two acres, one rood and twenty rods. He also received his share of further subdivisions of town land, made in 1643 and 1649 respectively. Micah Tompkins and his wife, Mary, were admitted December 12, 1643, to membership in a religious society in Milford. Their children were Jonathan, Elizabeth, baptized 1644 and married December 12, 1665, to James Bishop of New Haven, Conn., Daniel (who died aged two), Seth,

---

[58]Edward Tompkins, *A Record of the Ancestry and Kindred of the Children of Edward Tomkins Sr.* [Boston 1893], p. 39. Robert Bolton, *History of the Several Towns...of Westchester* [2nd ed, New York 1881], p. 233.

Lydia, Rebecca, Abigail, and Micah, all Biblical names. Bolton writes that it has been said Micah Tompkins secreted Goffe and Whalley for about two years from May 20th, 1661 [more likely June 11th], in the basement of a shop by his house in Milford.[59]

In May, 1666, Micah Tompkins was appointed one of a committee of eleven persons to purchase from the Indians a town site, where the city of Newark, New Jersey, now stands (which brings us back to Lawrence Ward). The deed for the land was obtained July 11, 1667. Micah Tompkins shared with the other original settlers in the property thus purchased, his home plot being located on the easterly side of Mulberry Street near corner of Kinney Street. In 1668 he was one of a committee charged with the duty of erecting a building to be used for religious services. The exact date of his death is not known, but it was sometime between June 30, 1688, the date of his will, and December, 1690, when his will was probated. His widow was living in 1695. Of particular interest is his connection (suggested by Bolton in his *History of Westchester*) to the Tompkins family of Pelham, associates of the Thomas Kirke who married into the Pell family (see above).[60] This is a far more telling connection than a putative relationship to the Kirkes of Quebec.

### Finally, William Goffe and Edward Whalley

If one looks in a standard biographical directory (or, for that matter, Wikipedia on line), one is likely to find an entry for Edward Whalley giving a birth date c. 1607 and a death date c. 1675 – while for

---

[59] *Ibid.*

[60] *Ibid.*

his son-in-law William Goffe one is likely to find a birth date c. 1605 and a death date c. 1679. What we know is that Edward Whalley's mother was Frances Cromwell, second wife of Richard Whalley – and Frances Cromwell's father was Sir Henry Cromwell of Hinchingbrooke (1524/1537-1604), a favorite of both Elizabeth and James I, and Frances Cromwell's mother was Joan Warren [1524-1584]. And the youngest (we believe) of their children was born in 1563. (Sir Henry's birthdate is now given as 1537, but his wife Joan Warren's is given as 1524, and his father's death date is given as 1533, which casts doubt on 1537 as his birthdate.[5661]) Even though Joan was a second wife, it is possible that Edward Whalley, even if he was her son, was born as early as the 1580s: we know his daughter Frances, who married William Goffe, was born in 1617. So goodbye to the 1607 birth-date for Whalley: it might be suggested 1593, for example, would be much more likely, though late (the 1605 date for Goffe could still hold)!

If Whalley was born around 1593 and died in 1677 or thereabouts (after a stroke circa 1675), and is buried at Hadley, and Goffe was born about 1605, when did he die? A preponderance of opinion gives 1679 or 1680 at Hadley, the legend of his burial in Dixwell's grave in New Haven being treated by assuming he was buried in that grave (on the New Haven Green, which was the old burial ground) nearly ten years before Dixwell was buried there. This seems improbable. Our family tradition is that he returned to Milford, and died there, at Simon's house. There is a third possibility – which, if this were detective fiction, at least might be considered.

There is an ambiguous figure in the story President Stiles tells, one Theophilus Whalley, of Virginia and Narragansett, Rhode Island

---

[61] [*The Peerage* 131119] [*The Peerage* 134024] [*The Peerage* 131121], online.

[1616?-1720?]. Some have argued he was really Edward Whalley, some that he was Edward's brother Robert Whalley. Theophilus disappears from Virginia, where he is well-attested, in 1679/1680, and turns up at Narragansett in 1680, where he is virtually unattested until a property transfer in 1710. Whether communications would permit it is uncertain, but the persistent rumors that Theophilus Whalley was a Regicide, and the high probability that Edward Whalley was dead, suggest the possibility that – if a Regicide -- this was William Goffe in hiding. Whether it was also the real Theophilus Whalley we can leave up to the detective story writer who might fashion a story out of this. The whole well-attested story of Theophilus Whalley does suggest, indeed, that truth is stranger than fiction – or very well could be.[62]

## Judges, Genealogy, History, Connecticut, and Commonwealth Men

We can see here that we are dealing pretty much with members of what we would today call the middle class (Lawrence Ward the elder) and the upper middle class, with considerable wealth, connections in some cases up and down the coast (arguably from Newfoundland to the Caribbean islands, certainly from Cambridge to Virginia), close family connections and other ties, particularly to Cromwell, with more distant ties even to the Royal family. We can see that Kellond and Kirke's "pursuit" was almost certainly designed to fail; we learn that the local "search" (likewise so designed) from the 14th of May (when Kellond and Kirke left) was called off on the 20th – but the Judges remained "in" their "Cave" until June 11th – perhaps to keep a lookout for the "Indians" or perhaps to keep a lookout on the Sound against the possibility of a ship

---

[62] Cora Lutz, "Ezra Stiles and the Legend of Hadley" in *Yale University Library Gazette* [1998], pp. 115-123

or ships from "Manhados" (and did the way in which the "basons" were left provide a signal or set of signals as to what was going on, or were there notes enclosed?)

The persistent connection between their leaving the cave and something to do with "Indians" may certainly be connected with the Indian troubles around Milford in the summer of 1661 – necessitating their going into the settlement – and as well with the lookout for the "Royalists" returning (corroborative detail to add verisimilitude to the narrative?) They left for Hadley in 1664, when Tompkins was involved in the move to Newark, and Simon Lobdell was on his way to Springfield (who possibly was all this time a citizen of Milford but making his rounds along the paths from New Haven to Hartford to Springfield or to Cambridge) – and perhaps one reason for the move to Hadley was the Royal capture of "Manhados" in 1664.

Theophilus Eaton had been King Charles's Minister in Denmark in 1633 (and Denmark was Charles's mother's country) and William Jones was Eaton's son-in-law and John Davenport his college roommate (and his house had nineteen chimneys). Daniel Gookin had fought in the Low Countries; his brother was M.P. in the Commonwealth Parliament, and he was involved with Cromwell's Caribbean schemes (and, by the way, he had survived Opechancanough's attack on Jamestown in 1622); Simon Lobdell's cousins were part of the Cromwellian settlement of Ireland (at Athenry and Mulpit and Derryowen) and his father is believed to have fought in the Dutch service (the family had ties with the Low Countries going back to Bernard de Loppedell [fl. 1381] and Waleran III of Luxembourg and even before).[63]

---

[63] J. C. Lobdell, "More Progress on Lobdell/Lopdell" in *Sussex Family Histor,* forthcoming 2018.

William Pierce, one of whose family commanded the *Hector*, bringing over Goffe and Whalley, was the Ferryman of the Atlantic, and Isaac Allerton of Plymouth and New Haven was one of his associates (and Mrs. Eyers's aunt who died in 1699 was the last alive of those who came over on the *Mayflower*, which Pierce later commanded). John Meigs (in Hammonassett in 1672) left his son a library including Foxe's *Book of Martyrs*, Ralegh's *Historie of the World*, Bacon's *Essays*, a Greek-English Lexicon and a Latin Dictionary; John Burrill (or Burwell) had an estate in Hemel Hempstead in Hertfordshire (and was descended from King Henry and the Fair Rosamonde).

This was a frontier, yes. But it was the westward part of the Atlantic commonwealth, and these were mostly gentlemen or yeomen adventurers of England – and by the way, the ties with Virginia and the Pilgrims were as strong as with the Puritans of Massachusetts Bay – except perhaps for those of the ambiguous third Major-General, Daniel Gookin of Massachusetts Bay. But also a Virginian, gentleman-adventurer, and Commonwealth man – and his was one of the first families in Virginia.

### For King or Cromwell? Can We Tell Without a Scorecard?

It may be late in time to suggest that the whole episode has been subject to misunderstanding, but it appears that Kellond and Kirke were not zealous royalists but in fact had Cromwellian connections – though in his Whitehill Prize Essay back in 1987, Douglas Wilson adopted the conventional attitude that they were "eager royalists."[64] He also, in company with almost every writer since the days when Fenimore

_____

[64] Douglas C. Wilson, "Web of Secrecy: Goffe, Whalley, and the Legend of Hadley" in *New England Quarterly* [1987], p. 515.

Cooper and Hawthorne sought to apply a thoroughly rationalist interpretation of the Angel of Hadley, argues for Goffe rather than Whalley as the Angel.[65] But that is another question – apart from the question of allegiances and connections, which is our present subject.

Kellond was a prosperous Boston merchant (richer than William Phips) – but also a family connection of Loyalist Governor Hutchinson, who collected the material on the Regicides, and wished to downplay any connection of his own family with rebellion against the King.[66] (Ironically, Goffe's diary and other papers that would have provided a more detailed account of the Judges in New England, were lost when the demonstrators opposing the Stamp Act burned Governor Hutchinson's house.) Kirke was almost certainly a well-connected Cromwellian (with later connections with Micah Tompkins, who hid the Judges in Milford).

The guide for the Judges was later a cousin-by-marriage of the Whalley family; one of the guides for Kellond and Kirke was in Blake's Navy (possibly with Nehemiah Bourne), the other the son of an emblematic Puritan, whose past guiding was for those in trouble with the English authorities. The searchers from Milford likewise had Cromwellian connections – which is what one would expect in Milford – though not so strong connections as Thomas Kirke's or even Simon Lobdell's. Actually, the better question is not "King or Cromwell?" – it's pretty much all Cromwell. The better question is now "England or New England?" and perhaps even "Crown or America?" It is at least

---

[65] George Dekker, "Sir Walter Scott, the Angel of Hadley, and American Historical Fiction" in *Journal of American Studies*, 17 [1983], pp. 219ff.

[66] Abigail Hutchinson, the Governor's aunt, married Thomas Kellond as her second husband, so he was the Governor's uncle by marriage (P. O. Hutchinson, ed., *Diary and Letters of Thomas Hutchinson,* London 1883, p. 32).

arguable that Judges' Cave is where the first drafts of the American Revolution were brewed.

# Epilogue or Appendix: The End of the Family Story

It was a famous story – the tale of Goffe and Whalley – from the day of Ezra Stiles to the days of Walter Scott and Fenimore Cooper and Nathaniel Hawthorne, till Hale's "The Man without a Country" replaced Hawthorne's "The Grey Champion" as America's emblematic story. But what came of it at last – and what is its value for us? There is one answer in the version in the author's possession, the family story that ends this way (take it as creative non-fiction, if not so good as Scott's or Hawthorne's or Fenimore Cooper's). The speaker, as noted before, is Simon Lobdell's grandson, Darius Lobdell, to his son, Jared Lobdell, in 1793.

"Save for certain aspects of his Lieutenancy at Springfield, and being admitted Freeman of Milford in Lord Oliver's day, my grandfather held no position of civil trust such as my father held, or I. But he was trusted with their lives by Edward Whalley, who governed five counties in England for his cousin Oliver, and by General Whalley's son-in-law William Goffe, who governed three and turned out Barebones' Parliament. And when our frontier moved to the westward and to the northward, and my grandfather grew to later middle age, he came back to Milford. He kept the Springfield property, though he sold the half-interest in Harvard's tavern he had from his brother Joseph in Massachusetts Bay. For thirty years his life was bound up with the Colonel's, and after the Colonel died, my grandfather lived nigh thirty years more. He was four-score and five when he died, and we had fought wars with the Indians to the eastward and with the Indians to the northward, wars with the French and with the Indians to the westward.

"There was a verse the Colonel remembered to my grandfather, and he to my father, and my father to me, though I am not sure I have it exactly: 'I have done one braver thing / Than all the Worthies did / And yet a braver thence doth spring / Which is, to keep that hid.' He that wrote it, the Colonel told my grandfather, was his own Reverend father's friend and his older brother's, him that went for a Papist, and my grandfather said he was told the poet was called both Puritan and Papist, but he was one of the old Queen's men and died or ever the Civil Wars began. My grandfather knew not the poet's name, but the Colonel would say, "'T is a quatrain well done, friend Simon, and d 'ye see, 't is of thee and me it speaks. Ay, 't is well done." And he would chuckle, at a joke my grandfather could not see, in the Nipmuck woods, or at Minister Russell's house in Hadley, or even in his last Ebenezer at Mill River.

"My grandfather did many brave things, and some of them I have told you, but I believe the Colonel was right. Bravest of all was the secret and good faith kept those thirty years, when Vermont was French country as our name tells you, and Hadley and Springfield were frontier towns, when the beaver was trapped in plenty along the Connecticut, and the Colonel learned his snap-shooting at my grandfather's side. Indeed and they were brave days."

A Commonwealth Man indeed! And so, it seems, were they all in New Haven then, those three centuries and a half ago. And they *were* brave days! [67]

---

[67] It is certainly likely, though not proven, that Goffe's family knew John Donne. In any case, it is important to remind ourselves, as by the quotation from Shakespeare that opens and the quotation from Donne that closes our story, that though their churchmanship differed, Whalley was born into Shakespeare's world and Goffe at least into Donne's – and by the way, their guide's grandfather fought against a different King Philip, in the days of the Armada. American history, as the Judges' story shows us, is not only *American* history.

# Bibliography

Abbott, Susan Woodruff, *Families of Early Milford Connecticut* [Baltimore 1979]

Banks, C. E., *Topographical Dictionary of 2885 English Emigrants to New England 1620-1650* [1937, reprinted Baltimore 2007]

Bates, A. C., ed.,*Records of the Particular Court of Connecticut 1639-1663* [Hartford 1928]

Bergen, Teunis G., *Genealogies of the State of New York*, Volume 1 [New York 1915], p. 235

Bolton, Robert, *History of the Several Towns, Manors, and Patents of the County of Westchester* [2nd edition, New York 1881]

Bremer, Francis J., *John Davenport: A Puritan in Three Worlds* [New Haven: Yale 2012]

Calder, Isabel M., *The New Haven Colony* [New Haven 1934]

Chapin, Orange, *The Chapin Genealogy* [Northampton 1862]

*Collections of the Massachusetts Historical Society*, Vol. XXVII (1836), p. 128. This is the volume with Gookin's *Christian Indians*

Cummings, A. L., "The Foster-Hutchinson House" in *Old-Time New England*, Vol. LIV [1964], pp. 59-61

Cutter, W. R., *New England Families, Genealogical and Memorial* [New York 1914]

*Dictionary of Canadian Biography* [on-line]

Dekker, George, "Sir Walter Scott, the Angel of Hadley, and American Historical Fiction" in *Journal of American Studies*, 17, 1983, pp. 219ff.

*Dictionary of National Biography* Vol. 22 (1890), pp. 152-164.

Gillespie, C. B., *Historic Record and Pictorial Description of the Town of Meriden* [Meriden 1907]

Gookin, Daniel, *Doings and Sufferings of the Christian Indians* [1677, published Boston 1836].

Hatch, C. E., Jr., *First Seventeen Years: Virginia 1607-1624* [Charlottesville/Jamestown 1957].

Hay, T. A., *Martin Genealogy* [New York 1911]

Hinman, Royal R., *A Catalogue of the Names of the Early Puritan Settlers of the Colony of Connecticut* [Hartford 1852]

*Historic Woodbridge: An Historic and Architectural Resource Survey* [Woodbridge CT 1994]

Hoadly, Charles J., *Records from the Colony or Jurisdiction of New Haven, from May 1653 to the Union* [Hartford 1858]

Howell, G. R., *Early History of Southampton, L.I.* [New York 1887]

Hutchinson, Peter O., ed., *Diary and Letters of Thomas Hutchinson,* [London 1883]

Lobdell, Jared, "The Dispersion of the Lobdell/Lopdell Family 1489-1705" in *Sussex Family History* [1977], pp. 81-84.

------------------. "More Progress on Lobdell/Lopdell" in *Sussex Family History*, forthcoming, 2018

------------------, "Progress on the Dispersion of the Lobdell/Lopdell Family in the 17th Century" in *Sussex Family History* (2002), pp. 42-51

Lobdell, Julia Harrison, *Simon Lobdell of Milford CT 1646* [Chicago 1907]

Lutz, Cora, "Ezra Stiles and the Legend of Hadley" in *Yale University Library Gazette* [1998], pp. 115-123

Malone, Patrick, *The Skulking Way of War: Technology and Tactics among the New England Indians* [Lanham MD 1991].

Mann, R. N. and C. C., *Camp-Kemp Family History* [Cedar Bluffs AL 1967];

McGhan, Judith, *Genealogies of Connecticut Families* from the *New England Historical and Genealogical Review* Volume II [Baltimore 1983]

Mead, Daniel, *History of the Town of Greenwich* [1857]

Merrick, Barbara Lambert, "Important Allerton-Brewster Connections" in *Mayflower Descendant*, Vol. 42 [1992], pp. 117ff

*N.Y. Genealogical and Biographical Record*, Vol. 51 [1920], p. 253 [Kellond's widow].

Nugent, Nell M., *Cavaliers and Pioneers: Abstracts of Virginia Land Patents and Grants 1623-1666* [Richmond 1934].

Sanford, Carlton, *Thomas Sanford, the Emigrant to New England* [Rutland VT 1911]

Savage, James, *Genealogical Dictionary of the First Settlers of New England* [Cambridge MA 1860].

Steiner, B. C., *History of Guilford and Madison CT* [1897 reprinted Guilford 1975]

Stiles, Ezra, *History of Three of the Judges of King Charles the First* [New Haven 1794]

Talcott, Alvan, *Families of Early Guilford Connecticut* [Baltimore 1984].

Torrey, C. A., *New England Marriages prior to 1700* [Baltimore 1985]

Trumbull, J. H., ed., *Public Records of the Colony of Connecticut*, Vol. 3 [Hartford 1859]

Versteeg, Dingman, ed., *Manhattan in 1628* [New York 1904].

Waters, Henry Fitzgilbert, *Genealogical Gleanings in England*, Volume 2 [Boston 1901 and Salem 1907 reprinted Baltimore 1969].

Wilson, Douglas C., "Web of Secrecy: Goffe, Whalley, and the Legend of Hadley" in *New England Quarterly* [1987]

Made in United States
Orlando, FL
02 May 2022

17409889R00041